Easy Thai Cooking

by A. Ujike

Foreword

The sweetness of palm sugar, the biting heat of chilies, the tartness of lime and the distinctive saltiness of fish sauce -- these flavors all together define the ethnic treat that is Thai cooking. Thai cooking creates a harmony between such various tastes as sweet and sour, hot, and smooth.

Not only is Thai food delicious, it is also healthy. Thai cooking is growing in popularity throughout the world. As a result, the ingredients used in Thai cooking are becoming more accessible not only in Asian supermarkets but in local markets as well. In this book, I introduce you to thirty authentic Thai dishes. I have selected these recipes because the ingredients called for in each recipe can generally be found in your local supermarket.

By Akiki Ujiie

© 1994 Parco Co., Ltd.

English Translation © 1998 by Heian International, Inc.

Translation by Dianne Ooka, Edited by Monique Sugimoto

With thanks to Great Kitchen Thai Restaurant, Los Angeles, California, USA

Heian International, Inc.
1815 West 205th Street, Suite #301
Torrance, CA 90501

E-MAIL: heianemail@heian.com • WEB SITE: www.heian.com

First American Edition 1998
98 99 00 01 02 03 04 05 9 8 7 6 5 4 3 2 1

ISBN: 0-89346-841-X

Notes about Thai Cooking

Mortar & Pestle

When it is time to cook, the mortar is brought out and the necessary spices, chilies and other ingredients are pounded. The mortar and pestle are so important  to Thai cooking that the flavor of the meal can be gauged by the sound of the mortar and pestle. Pounding and crushing spices in a mortar seems to bring out the natural flavor of spices and other condiments. If a mortar is not available, a blender can be used.

Eating Utensils

Unlike other Asian countries where chopsticks are used, food is usually eaten with a spoon in Thailand. Generally, the spoon is held in the right hand and the fork is held in the left hand. Since steaks and other large entrees requiring a cutting knife are not part of Thai cooking, knives are not usually necessary. From eating rice and curries to making the entrée portions a little smaller, a spoon is the most adequate utensil when eating Thai food.

Alcohol and Thai Food

Almost any kind of liquor goes with Thai food. Beer, however, seems to be more suitable than other alcoholic beverages. Thai beer has an alcohol content that is higher than most American beers. A popular brand of Thai beer is Singha Beer. There are also beers with low alcohol content such as Singha Gold. If wine is more to your liking, a dry wine also goes quite nicely with Thai food. For a non-alcoholic beverage, cold Chinese tea or the like is recommended.

Table of Contents

*Recipes are for four servings unless otherwise indicated

Dishes for any Dinner Menu

Unlike European meals, Thai meals do not start with an appetizer and end with a dessert. Meals generally consist of several dishes including soups, salads and a main dish, all of which are served at the same time. The dishes are placed in the center of the table and everyone takes as much as they like from each of the dishes. Here are seven delicious dishes that may be served as part of your evening meal. The flavor and fragrance of these dishes will add an ethnic twist to your menu and will surely become your family's favorites.

Spicy Beef Salad
(Yam-Nua)

*Marinated beef and vegetables tossed in a spicy dressing
make up this sumptuous salad.*

Ingredients

10 ounces beef fillet
½ red onion, thinly sliced
8 cherry tomatoes, halved
½ stalk celery, thinly sliced into 2" pieces
1 pickling cucumber, sliced in half lengthwise, then
thinly on diagonal into 2" pieces
5-6 mushrooms, thinly sliced

Marinade
a) 1 tablespoon fish sauce
   1½ teaspoon seasoning sauce
   1 clove garlic, grated

Dressing
b) 1-2 coriander roots, minced
   1 clove garlic, grated
   2 large Thai chilies, minced
   (or 1 teaspoon of crushed red pepper)
c) 2 teaspoons sugar
   2½ teaspoons lemon juice
   2½ teaspoons fish sauce

Directions

1 Mix a) and add beef. Marinate in mixture for 10-15 minutes.
2 Grill or fry meat until slightly browned or to taste. Remove from heat. When cool, slice on a slant into ⅜" pieces.
3 Grind b) in a mortar. Add c) and mix well.
4 Combine the sliced beef and vegetables in a bowl. Toss with the dressing and serve.

Vegetables and meat cut to appropriate sizes.

Lightly fried meat cut on a slant.

Using a mortar to prepare the dressing.

Spicy Noodle Salad (Yam Whoon Sen)

This noodle salad is made with noodles, shrimp, chicken, pork and vegetables.

Ingredients

4 ounces dried mungbean noodles
8 medium shrimp with tails, shelled and deveined
2 chicken breast fillets
3½ ounces ground pork
¼ red onion, thinly sliced
1 stalk celery, thinly sliced and leaves chopped
3 teaspoons dried shrimp
½ ounce dried wood ears
vegetable oil

Dressing

a) 1-2 coriander roots, minced
     1 clove garlic, grated
     8 small Thai chilies, minced
     (or 1 teaspoon crushed red pepper)

b) 2 teaspoons sugar
     2½ tablespoons lemon juice
     2-3 tablespoons fish sauce
     1 tablespoon chili sauce

Directions

1 Soak noodles in water for 10 minutes. Add to boiling water and cook briefly. Drain, rinse and cut to desired lengths.
2 Poach chicken then cook shrimp in boiling water. When cool, cut each shrimp into thirds and slice chicken into thin pieces.
3 Fry pork in an unoiled frypan.
4 Saute dried shrimp lightly.
5 Soak wood ears in water. When soft, cut into bite-sized pieces.
6 Crush a) in a mortar then add b). Mix well.
7 Place all ingredients in a bowl. Toss with the dressing and serve.

Preparing the ingredients in advance.

Using a mortar to prepare the dressing.

Chicken Sautéed with Beefsteak Basil (Gai Phad Baikapow)

This chicken and vegetable dish flavored with curry paste and fish sauce is wonderful alone or over rice.
The basil garnish makes it a particularly fragrant delight.

Ingredients

14 ounces chicken thighs, skinned, deboned and cut into small pieces
2 ounce can shimeji mushrooms
8 cherry tomatoes
½ red bell pepper, cut lengthwise into thin strips
½ red onion, thinly sliced
2 cloves garlic, thinly sliced
15 large leaves beefsteak basil
1-2 ounces red curry paste
1½ tablespoons fish sauce
1½ teaspoons sugar
vegetable oil for deep frying
3½ tablespoons vegetable oil for sautéeing

Directions

1 Heat oil reserved for deep frying. Add basil leaves a few at a time. Deep fry until crisp. In the same oil, deep fry onion then garlic. Set aside.
2 Heat remaining oil in a frypan. Add curry paste and cook. When fragrant and color has changed, add chicken.
3 When chicken is almost done, add mushrooms, tomatoes, peppers and continue cooking.
4 Add fish sauce and sugar. Adjust flavor to taste.
5 Place in a serving dish. Garnish with fried basil, garlic, onion and serve.

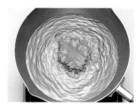

Fry each of the fragrant ingredients separately.

Adjusting curry to taste.

Marinated Beef and Noodles (Kuai-Tiao Phat See Ew)

This is a delicious fried noodle dish featuring marinated beef and greens.

Ingredients

10 ounces dried rice noodles
7 ounces beef, thinly sliced
2 tablespoons Tenmenjan
1 tablespoon light soy sauce
8 tablespoons vegetable oil
1 clove garlic, minced
7 ounces broccoli or mustard greens

Marinade
1 tablespoon miso paste
2 tablespoons oyster sauce
Pepper
½ tablespoon cornstarch

Directions

1 Mix marinade ingredients and add beef. Marinate for 10-15 minutes.
2 Add noodles to boiling water and cook until al dente.
3 Heat 4 tablespoons of the oil in a wok. Add noodles and stir fry. Add Tenmenjan and soy sauce. When noodles are coated with sauce, remove to a serving plate.
4 Heat remaining oil and add garlic. When fragrant, add meat and sauté.

5 When meat is about half done, add greens and stir-fry for another 1-2 minutes.
6 Place meat on top of noodles and toss to mix.

Thinly sliced beef is prepared for marinade.

Adding greens when meat is half done.

Fried Shrimp Patties
(Thot Man Kung)

*Finely minced shrimp and fragrant ingredients make these fried
shrimp patties a dish your whole family will enjoy.*

Ingredients

10 ounces shrimp, heads and tails removed,
shelled and deveined
½ cup coriander leaves cut in ⅜" pieces
1 egg yolk, beaten
bread crumbs
vegetable oil for deep frying
Thai chili sauce (or basic chili sauce recipe below)

Paste

1 clove garlic, grated
½ teaspoon coarsely ground black pepper
1 tablespoon fish sauce or light soy sauce
1 teaspoon salt
pinch of sugar

Directions

1 Combine paste ingredients and mix until a paste is
formed.
2 Wash and dry shrimp with a paper towel. Chop
then crush until a paste is formed.
3 Combine 1) and 2) with the coriander and mix
well. Shape into patties about 2" in diameter and ½"
thick. (Coat hands with salad oil to make shaping
patties easier.)
4 Dip patties in egg yolk then coat with bread crumbs.
Deep fry until golden brown.
5 Serve with Thai chili sauce.

> ### Basic Chili Sauce
> 1 cucumber, thinly sliced
> ¼ red onion, thinly
> sliced
> Several peanuts,
> roughly chopped
> ½ cup vinegar
> 2 tablespoons sugar
> ½ teaspoon salt
>
> Mix ingredients
> thoroughly.

*Using a cleaver to prepare
shrimp.*

Mixing coriander and shrimp.

*Shrimp patties before and
after breading.*

Fragrant Pan-Fried Fish (Pla Yang)

Flavored with Thai seasonings and spices and served with a tasty sauce, this is a wonderful way to serve any white fish in season.

Ingredients

4 white-fleshed fish (such as snapper, perch, rock cod etc.)
4 tablespoons vegetable oil
20 coriander leaves

Paste

a) 4 cloves garlic
    4-5 coriander roots
    40-50 black peppercorns
b) 5 tablespoons fish sauce

Sauce

3½ tablespoons fish sauce
1 small Thai chili (or 1 teaspoon crushed red pepper)
several mint leaves, minced
3½ tablespoons lemon juice

Directions

1 Grind a) in a mortar. Add b) and mix until a paste is formed.
2 Gut, clean and scale fish. Make several scores on each side of fish.
3 Rub paste onto fish, including the insides.
Let sit for 15 minutes. Divide coriander into four equal portions. Stuff fish with coriander.

4 Heat oil in a frypan. Fry fish until both sides are golden brown. (Or wrap in aluminum foil and bake in 350° - 400° oven for 20-30 minutes.) Transfer to a platter.
5 Combine sauce ingredients and mix well. Pour over fish and serve.

Preparing the paste in a mortar.

Fish rubbed with paste and stuffed with coriander leaves.

Rubbing paste over fish to get full flavor.

Fragrant Steamed Fish (Pla Neung)

This steamed fish is made with fragrant vegetables, pickled plums and pork.
It is served with an authentic Thai sauce.

Ingredients

1 white-fleshed fish (such as perch or tile fish)

a) 1 green onion, cut lengthwise into 2" pieces
     3 large Thai chilies, cut lengthwise into thin
     strips (or ½ bell pepper)
     2" piece ginger, cut lengthwise into thin strips
     3 medium shiitake mushrooms, cut length-
     wise into thin strips
      ½ ounce lean pork, cut lengthwise
     1 pickled plum, rinsed and pit removed

b) 3 tablespoons light soy sauce
     1 tablespoon seasoning sauce

Covering fish with vegetables.

Directions

1 Gut, clean and scale fish. Make several scores on each side of fish then place on a platter.
2 Put pork in scored areas and green onion inside fish. Arrange remaining ingredients of a) on top of fish.
3 Bring water in a steamer to a boil. Place platter in steamer, cover and steam 15-30 minutes. (Time will vary depending on size of fish.)
4 When done, pour b) over fish and steam for another 1-2 minutes. Serve immediately. (When removing platter from steamer, be careful not to spill juices.)

Pouring sauce over steamed fish.

Easy Curries and Soups

Curries are among the most popular of Thai foods. A special feature of Thai curry is the use of coconut milk. The smoothness of coconut combined with the penetrating heat of curry spices makes Thai curry delicious. Another popular dish in Thai cooking is, without a doubt, Tom Yam Kung soup. Here are three easy curries and a Tom Yam Kung recipe for a taste of Thai cooking's most representative dishes.

Red Curry with Beef and Pumpkin (Kaeng Nua Sai Fak Thong)

This flavorful hot and spicy dish combines the sweetness of pumpkin, the heat of chilies, and the soothing coolness of coconut milk.

Ingredients

10 ounces beef or chicken thigh, thinly sliced
¼ small pumpkin, cut into ¾" pieces
14 ounce can coconut milk
1⅔ ounces red curry paste
4 lime leaves (or 1 bunch holy basil or sweet basil)
2-3 tablespoons fish sauce
1 red bell pepper, cut lengthwise into thin strips
2 tablespoons vegetable oil
2 cups water
Garnish: mint leaf

Directions

1 Heat oil in a pot. Add curry paste, and cook briefly over low heat.
2 When fragrant, add coconut milk. Raise heat to medium.
3 When oil rises to the surface, add meat and cook.
4 When meat is about half way done, add water, pumpkin and fish sauce and lower heat. (Cooking over high heat will cause pumpkin to break apart.)
5 Taste and adjust flavors if necessary. Add pepper and lime leaves. Bring to a boil then remove from heat. Garnish and serve.

Sautéeing red curry paste until fragrant.

Oil rising to the surface when heating coconut milk mixture.

Basil and red pepper add color to the dish.

Green Curry with Eggplant and Chicken (Kaeng Khiew Wan)

A deliciously mild curry that is both sweet and spicy. This curry is sure to please everyone.

Ingredients

1 pound chicken thighs, boned and cut into bite size pieces
3 oriental eggplants, skinned and cut into 2" pieces
1 pack shimeji mushrooms, halved
10 green peppers, cut in half diagonally
1 red bell pepper, cut lengthwise into thin strips
1½-2 ounces green curry paste
2 cups coconut milk
6 lime leaves (or 1 bunch holy basil or sweet basil)
2 tablespoons vegetable oil
1¼ cup water

a) 1½ teaspoons fish sauce
    1 tablespoon sugar

*For a more authentic flavor, add a small amount of ground cumin and coriander to a).

Directions

1 Heat oil in a pot. Add curry paste and cook briefly over low heat.
2 When fragrant, add coconut milk. Cook over medium heat until oil rises to the surface. Add chicken.
3 When chicken is partially done, add water, eggplant, mushrooms and half of the lime leaves.
4 When chicken is fully cooked, add a). Taste and adjust flavor if necessary.
5 Add green and red peppers and bring to a boil briefly then remove from heat. Garnish with remaining lime leaves and serve.

Cooking coconut milk until oil rises to the surface.

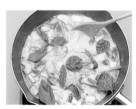

Bell peppers added for color.

Rice Noodles with Mackerel Curry and Vegetables (Khanom Jin Nam Ya)

This curry sauce made with grilled mackerel, coconut milk, and spices makes a great topping for rice noodles.

Ingredients

6 bundles rice noodles
1 medium mackerel
1¾ ounces panang or red curry paste
2 cups coconut milk
⅔ cup water
a) ¼ red onion, minced
   1 clove garlic, minced
b) 2 dried galangal roots
   5-6 pieces rhizome
   3 tablespoons dried lemon grass
   2-3 dried lime leaves
c) 2 tablespoons fish sauce
   1 teaspoon salt

1 cup bean sprouts, roots removed and blanched
½ cucumber, seeded and cut into matchsticks
2 pieces of pickled mustard cabbage, cut into strips
½ red bell pepper, cut lengthwise into thin strips
5 leaves beef steak basil, cut into ¼" pieces

Directions

1 Cut mackerel into 3 pieces. Grill over open flame. Remove skin and break into small pieces. Set aside.
2 Soak b) in water for 10 minutes. Mince finely.
3 Put coconut milk and water in a pot and bring to boil. Add curry paste. When fragrant, add fish and both a) and b). Cook for a few minutes longer.

4 When entire mixture is fragrant, mix in a blender for 30 seconds.
5 Return mixture to pot and add c). Correct flavor. (Flavor should be a bit strong.)
6 Cook rice noodles in boiling water to al dente. Do not overcook. Drain and let cool. Create bite size portions by wrapping noodles around your fingers.
7 Arrange basil, vegetables and noodles on a platter and serve with the curry.

Cooked mackerel and dried ingredients after soaking in water.

Blending coconut milk mixture.

Winding noodles around fingers to make single servings.

Hot and Salty Shrimp Soup
(Tom Yam Kung)

Made from scratch or with shrimp paste, the various flavors in this soup are sure to make this dish a popular one.

Ingredients

1¾ ounces shrimp soup paste (or 1 cube of shrimp soup base)
2 cups water
8 medium shrimp, heads removed, shelled and deveined
½ can rice straw mushrooms, cut in half
Garnish: coriander leaves

Use following seasonings in amounts as desired to taste:
lemon juice
fish sauce
sugar
chili in oil

To make shrimp stock from scratch, use the following ingredients in lieu of shrimp paste and water:
3 cups chicken stock
4 fresh lime leaves, torn into small pieces
2 tablespoons fresh lemon grass, cut diagonally and pounded with back of knife
4 small Thai chilies, crushed
3 pieces galangal, lightly scored

Directions

1 Heat water in a pot. Add shrimp paste and stir until well blended.
2 Add mushrooms and bring to a boil. Add seasoning ingredients to taste.
3 When desired flavor is obtained, add shrimp and return to a boil.
4 Remove from heat immediately. Garnish and serve.

(If making home-made soup stock, combine stock ingredients in a pot and bring to a boil. Continue with recipe from step 2.)

Ingredients used it making soup from scratch.

Bringing to a boil after adding shrimp.

Recipes For a Thai Twist on Omelets, Rice and Noodles

Thai cooking isn't made up solely of hot dishes.In addition to the curries and chilies, there are a wealth of other popular seasonings that give Thai food its distinctive flavor. The following recipes make use of other common Thai ingredients to give egg, rice and noodle dishes a Thai flavor.

Ground Pork Omelet (Khai Jiew Mousap)

Thai seasonings give this omelet a whole new flavor.

Ingredients

4 eggs
2½ ounces ground pork
1½ tablespoons fish sauce
1 teaspoon seasoning sauce
3½ tablespoons vegetable oil
Thai chili sauce
Garnish: coriander leaves (or spring onion), chopped;
several slices red bell pepper

Directions

1 Break eggs into a bowl and beat. Add ground pork, fish sauce and seasoning sauce. Mix well.
2 Heat oil in a wok or frying pan. Pour egg mixture into frypan. Shape into an omelet and cook. When bottom is slightly browned, turn over and cook until edges are crisp. Remove from heat.
3 Garnish with chili sauce, coriander and red pepper.

Red peppers and coriander for garnish.

Egg mixture with ground pork and seasonings.

Pineapple Fried Rice (Khao Phad Sapparod)

This fried rice dish made with pineapple, ham, shrimp, and raisins will tempt even the most jaded palate.

Ingredients

1 ripe pineapple
12 small shrimp, heads removed, shelled and deveined
3 tablespoons vegetable oil
1 clove garlic, minced

a) 5-6 slices ham, cubed into d" pieces
    2 medium onions, roughly chopped
    5 small carrots, roughly chopped
b) 2 tablespoons fish sauce
    1 teaspoon black pepper

3 cups cooked rice
2 red bell peppers, roughly chopped
3 tablespoons raisins
Garnish: green onion, chopped; peanuts, roughly chopped

4 When just about cooked, add pineapple, peppers, and raisins and cook briefly.
5 Remove excess juice from pineapple shell with a paper towel. Line shell with plastic wrap and add rice mixture.
6 Garnish and serve.

Carefully carving out center of pineapple.

Adding pineapple to finished dish.

Directions

1 Cut pineapple in half. With a carving knife, carefully remove flesh. Cut into ⅜" cubes.
2 Heat oil in a frying pan. Add garlic and sauté. When fragrant, add a) and continue sautéeing.
3 Add shrimp and b). Taste and adjust flavor according to taste. Add rice and continue sautéeing.

Thai Fried Noodles (Phad Thai)

Shrimp, chicken, pickled radish and fried tofu, make up this noodle dish.
The condiments served with this dish give these noodles a truly Thai flavor.

Ingredients

10 ounces dried rice noodles

a) 12 small shrimp,
heads removed,
shelled and deveined
(or 3½ ounces pork,
thinly sliced)
5¼ ounces chicken,
thinly sliced
1 tablespoon pickled
radish, minced
½ fried tofu cake, cut
into small pieces

3½ tablespoons water
2 eggs
bean sprouts and leeks
to taste
vegetable oil

b) 2 tablespoons vinegar
4 teaspoons sugar
2 tablespoons light
soy sauce
3 teaspoons chili
sauce
3 teaspoons ketchup

Garnish:
peanuts, roughly
chopped
lemon wedges

Condiments:
fish sauce with chili
crushed pepper
sugar
vinegar

Directions

1 Soak noodles in water for 15 minutes. Drain and set aside.
2 Make two servings at a time. Heat oil in frying pan and add ½ of a).
3 Add ½ of the noodles and continue to cook. Add ½ of b) and mix well.
4 Move the ingredients to one side of the pan and add more oil. Cook one egg in the oil then stir into mixture. (Egg can be cooked in advance then added.)
5 Just before turning off heat, add half of the vegetables and cook briefly.
6 Repeat 1-5 for remaining servings. Garnish and serve with condiments.

Prepare ingredients in advance.

Draining water from noodles in a strainer.

Cooking egg in one side of the frypan.

Fried Stuffed Chicken Wings (Pek Kai Yad Sai)

Stuffed with noodles and pork, this recipe gives a new way to serve chicken wings.
These chicken wings make a great appetizer.

Ingredients 5 servings
10 chicken wings
½ ounce mungbean noodles

a) 3½ ounces ground pork
   ½ cup coriander leaves, roughly chopped
   ¼ ounce wood ears, softened in water then
   chopped
vegetable oil for deep frying

Seasoning
½ tablespoon ground coriander powder
½ clove garlic, minced
½ teaspoon black pepper
½ tablespoon fish sauce
½ teaspoon seasoning sauce

Sauce
sweet chili sauce

Directions
1 Rinse chicken wings in water. Insert fingers into cut end of wing, and carefully remove the two bones. Set aside.
2 Soak noodles in cold water for 10 minutes. Add to boiling water and cook briefly. Drain, rinse and cut to desired lengths.
3 Combine a), seasoning ingredients and noodles. Mix well.

4 Stuff chicken wings with mixture.
5 Heat oil to 340° F and fry wings until golden brown. (When the opening of the wings begins to close up, this is a sign that the stuffing is cooked.)
6 Arrange on a platter and serve with sweet chili sauce.

Prepare ingredients in advance.

Breaking wings at joint to remove bones.

Working bones loose to form a pocket.

Chicken wings before cooking.

Delicious Thai Desserts

From smooth to sticky and plain to sweet, Thai desserts are filled with many different textures and tastes. The colorfulness and unique sweetness of coconut milk used in desserts make Thai desserts even more appealing. No matter how full you find yourself after a meal, you'll just want to have one of these delicious desserts.

Fried Bananas and Coconut (Guoy Tod)

This crisp "melt-in-your-mouth" dessert combines bananas with the sweetness of coconut.

Ingredients

3 bananas, sliced into ⅜" pieces
¾ can coconut milk (14 ounce can)
1 cup grated coconut
½ teaspoon salt
½ cup sugar
3 tablespoons roasted white sesame seeds
½ tablespoon baking powder
1 scant cup flour
vegetable oil for deep frying
Toppings: cinnamon; granulated sugar

Directions

1 Place all ingredients in a bowl and mix well.
2 Heat oil to 350° F. Using a spoon, form balls of the mixture and fry in the oil until golden brown.
3 Sprinkle with toppings to taste and serve.

Mixing all ingredients in a bowl.

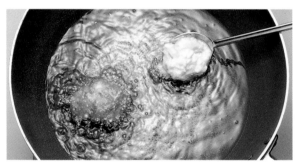

Spooning mixture into oil and cooking until golden brown.

Tapioca with Coconut Syrup
(Toptim Krob)

This colorful tapioca dessert is as pleasing to the eye as it is to the palate.

Ingredients

½ can tapioca (20 ounce can packed in water)
cornstarch
food coloring (2 colors as desired)
Optional: crushed ice

Syrup
½ can coconut milk (14 ounce can)
14 ounces water
1¾ cups sugar
1 teaspoon salt

Directions

1 Drain tapioca and cut into ¼" cubes.
2 In two separate bowls, mix food colorings with water. Place ⅓ of the tapioca in one color and ⅓ in the other color. (Leave remaining a as is.)
3 Put all tapioca in a strainer and rinse under cold water. Transfer to a bowl and add cornstarch. Mix until tapioca is well coated.
4 Add tapioca to boiling water. When cornstarch coating becomes clear, remove tapioca with a slotted spoon. Run under cold water until cool.
5 Place syrup ingredients in a pot and bring to a boil. Remove from heat and let cool.
6 Drain excess water from tapioca and place in serving dishes. Top with syrup and crushed ice and serve.

Coloring tapioca in desired colors.

Boil tapioca in a pot large enough for tapioca to move easily.

Coconut Milk and Egg Gelatin (Wun Gati)

This mildly sweet and cooling gelatin dessert brings to mind a gentle tropical breeze.

Ingredients 8-12 servings

Top Layer
¼ ounce powdered gelatin
2¼ cups water
¾ cup sugar
1 egg, beaten

Bottom layer
¼ ounce gelatin
2¼ cups water

a) 1 bag coconut milk powder (2 ounce size)
    ½ tablespoon fine rice flour
    ½ teaspoon salt
    1 cup sugar

Garnish: mint

Directions

1 Prepare the top layer first. Place gelatin and water in a saucepan and bring to a boil.
2 When disolved, add sugar. When sugar is fully dissolved remove from heat. Slowly add egg to mixture.
3 Pour mixture into ring mold and refrigerate.
4 Repeat step 1 to prepare gelatin for the bottom layer.
5 Add a) to the gelatin and continue cooking.
6 While mixture is still hot and the refrigerated gelatin is solid, pour it into the mold. (If mixture is allowed to cool, the top and bottom layers will separate.) Refrigerate until completely cooled.
7 Flip onto a serving plate and cut into individual portions. Garnish and serve.

Egg added to gelatin.

Top layer made first.

Bottom layer made second.

Sweet Basil and Fruit with Syrup (Polamai Roikaew)

This colorful melange of fruits in a sweet syrup makes a great light dessert and is reminiscent of a nice fruit punch.

Ingredients
1 tablespoon sweet basil seeds
¾ cup water

Syrup
1 cup sugar
1 cup water

Fruit
fruits in season, cubed (kiwi, strawberries, mango, shown here)

Topping: rum or lemon juice

Sweet basil seeds before (upper right) and after (bottom right) adding water.

Directions
1 Combine the ¾ cup of water with the basil seeds. Allow seeds to soften and expand. (Seeds should soften in about three minutes.)
2 Mix the syrup ingredients in a pot and bring to a boil. When thickened, remove from heat and let cool.
3 Add fruit and sweet basil seeds to syrup.
4 Top with a small amount of rum or lemon juice and serve.

Tapioca Pudding (Saku Piak)

This dessert combines the sweetness of coconut and brown sugar syrup with the distinctive texture of tapioca.

Ingredients

5¼ ounces small pearl tapioca
¼ ounce powdered gelatin mixed with 2 tablespoons of water (or one egg white, stiffly beaten)
1¼ ounces sugar

Coconut Sauce
2¼ ounces coconut milk powder
¼ cup boiling water
pinch of salt

Topping: brown sugar syrup

Use plenty of water to boil tapioca.

Mixing tapioca with egg and sugar.

Placing tapioca in pudding molds.

Directions

1 Place tapioca in a strainer and rinse under cold water.
2 Bring a pot of water to a boil. Add tapioca and cook for about 10 minutes. Cover pot and steam for another 10 minutes.
3 When tapioca is transparent, drain water and rinse. Add gelatin and sugar immediately and mix well.
4 Pour into pudding molds and refrigerate.
5 Dissolve coconut powder in boiling water. Add salt.
6 Turn hardened tapioca into serving dishes and add coconut sauce. Top with brown sugar syrup and serve.

Mango Sherbet (Itim Mamuang)

This delicious sherbet with a hint of rum makes a wonderfully refreshing dessert.

Ingredients

1 pound fresh or frozen mango

a)   3½ tablespoons rum or lemon juice
     3½ ounces sugar
     ½ cup water
     1 egg white, stiffly beaten

Garnish: mint

Mixing mango, rum and sugar in a blender.

Use a good mixing bowl to mix ingredients.

Directions

1 Combine mango and a) in a blender and mix thoroughly.
2 Pour mixture into a bowl and place in the refrigerator.
3 When mixture begins to harden, stir briefly with a wire whisk and refrigerate again.
4 Repeat step 3 two to three more times. On the third (or final) time, add egg white. (The entire procedure takes about 2 hours.)
5 Scoop the sherbet into serving dishes. Garnish and serve.

Adding egg white at end of process.

Pumpkin and Coconut Milk (Fak Thong Kaeng Buat)

The tenderness of pumpkin and the sweetness of coconut milk make up this healthy and simple dessert.

Ingredients

¼ pumpkin, cut into ½" pieces
½ can coconut milk (14 ounce can)
1½ cups water
1 cup sugar
¾ teaspoon salt

Directions

1 Put water in a saucepan and bring to a boil. Add remaining ingredients and lower heat.
2 Continue to cook over low heat until pumpkin is soft. (Cooking over high heat will cause pumpkin to break apart.)
3 Spoon into serving dishes and serve.

Coconut and pumpkin alone make up this easy dessert.

A Menu of Easy Thai Dishes For a Dazzling Luncheon

Here is a menu of dishes, each with its own unique flavor, that is sure to make any luncheon a hit. The combination of these dishes, from the dipping sauces and vegetables to the shish kebabs, brings out the natural charm and wonder that is Thai cooking.

Rice Cakes with Coconut Sauce (Khao Tang Na Tang)

Deep fried rice cakes and a sweet and sour coconut sauce make up this crunchy dish. It can be served with a meal or as a snack.

Ingredients

20 rice cakes
vegetable oil for deep frying
Garnish: coriander leaves (or green onions)
red bell pepper, top cut off and contents removed

Coconut Sauce
1 can coconut milk (14 ounce can)
2 teaspoons crushed red pepper
2 tablespoons unsweetened peanut butter

a) 3½ ounces shrimp, minced
    3½ ounces ground pork
    1 clove garlic, minced
    ¼ red onion, minced
    2 tablespoons palm sugar
    2 tablespoons fish sauce
    1½ tablespoons tamarind juice (or lemon juice)

Directions

1 Heat oil and add rice cakes a few at a time. Fry until puffy and browned on both sides.
2 Pour coconut milk in saucepan and heat. When oil rises to the surface, add pepper and cook until fragrant and red in color.

3 Add a) to the saucepan and cook. When done, add peanut butter and bring to a boil. Adjust flavor if necessary.
4 Pour sauce into shelled bell pepper or serving dish. Garnish and serve with rice cakes.

Cooking tamarind to extract juice or use lemon juice.

Boiling sauce ingredients.

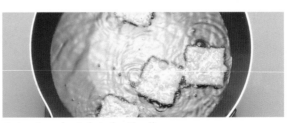
Frying rice cakes in hot oil until puffy.

Spicy Papaya Salad (Som Tam)

*This salad is representative of cooking in northeastern Thailand.
If papaya isn't available, carrots make a nice substitute.*

Ingredients

10 ounces unripe papaya, cut into strips
7-8 green beans, cut into 1" pieces
7-8 cherry tomatoes, halved
6 tablespoons dried shrimp, softened in warm water
1 clove garlic
1 small Thai chili, minced (or equivalent amount of crushed red pepper)
1½ tablespoons lemon juice
1½ tablespoons fish sauce
1 tablespoon palm sugar

Topping: 1 tablespoon peanuts, roughly chopped

Grinding garlic, dried shrimp and chili.

Directions

1 Place the shrimp, garlic and chili in a mortar and grind. Add papaya, green beans, cherry tomatoes along with the lemon juice, fish sauce and palm sugar. Mix until well blended.
2 When the vegetables become soft, place on a serving platter. Top with peanuts and serve.

Vegetables added to mortar to finish salad.

Seafood and Vegetables Wrapped in Lettuce (Mieng Kom)

Seven different ingredients and a distinctive sauce make up these delightful Thai tacos.

Ingredients

Sauce
¼ cup dried shrimp
1 tablespoon shrimp paste
½ cup water
1 cup palm sugar
2 tablespoons fish sauce
¼ cup grated coconut

Filling
1 cup grated coconut
¼ cup chopped red onion
¼ cup peeled and chopped ginger
¼ cup peanuts
¼ cup dried shrimp
¼ cup cubed lime or lemon
small Thai chilis, chopped
green or red lettuce leaves

Directions

1 Start by preparing the sauce. Soak the dried shrimp in water for 5 minutes. Drain and squeeze out excess water. Grind to a powder in a mortar or blender.
2 Grill the shrimp paste until lightly browned. Set aside.

3 Roast grated coconut in an unoiled frying pan until lightly browned, and set aside.
4 Combine the water and palm sugar in a saucepan and heat. Add the shrimp paste and fish sauce and simmer.
5 When the mixture thickens, add ground shrimp and roasted coconut. Boil for about one minute.
6 Place the filling ingredients in separate serving dishes. Put sauce in a bowl and arrange lettuce on a platter.
7 Fill lettuce leaves with filling ingredients. Add sauce and eat.

Roasting coconut flakes for sauce and filling at the same time.

Cool sauce until slightly thickened. Sauce will harden when cooled.

Pork Satay with Special Sauce (Mu Satay)

The marinade and dipping sauces make these Thai shish kebabs a wonderful treat.

Ingredients

5 ounces pork loin, cut into ¾" strips

Marinade
2 tablespoons coconut milk
ground tumeric
1½ teaspoons condensed milk
salt and pepper

Basting sauce
coconut cream, small amount
ground turmeric, small amount

bamboo skewers

toasted bread cut into squares

Dipping sauce
2 tablespoons curry paste
¼ cup unsweetened peanut butter
1 tablespoon ground coriander
¾ can coconut milk (14 ounce can)
2 tablespoons sugar
fish sauce, small amount

Salad ingredients
½ cucumber, cut into rounds, then halved
¼ red onion, thinly sliced
1 red pepper (or bell pepper), minced
6 tablespoons sugar
4 tablespoons vinegar
½ teaspoon salt
4 tablespoons boiling water

Directions

1 Bring coconut to a boil in a saucepan to prepare marinade. Add remaining marinade ingredients and cook for 5 minutes. Remove from heat and let cool.
2 Add pork to marinade and refrigerate for half a day.
3 Combine basting ingredients.
4 Skewer strips of meat and grill. Baste occasionally during cooking.
5 Combine dipping sauce ingredients in a saucepan and cook for about 3 minutes.
6 Mix the salad ingredients.
7 Arrange sauce and skewers on a platter with small pieces of toast.
8 Dip pork and toast in sauces to eat. Use skewers to eat salad.

Marinating pork in marinade.

Basting shish kebabs.

Ground Meat Salad (Lapp Issan)

*This popular Thai salad combines ground meat and vegetables
in a flavorful mixture.*

Ingredients

7 ounces ground pork
2 tablespoons uncooked rice
1 tablespoon water
1 teaspoon crushed red pepper
2 tablespoons lemon juice
1½ tablespoons fish sauce
½ red onion, thinly sliced
2-3 pieces spring onion, cut into ⅜" lengths
1 cup coriander leaves, cut into ⅜" pieces
endive (or cabbage)
chicory

Garnish: mint

Directions

1 Put ground pork and the water in an unoiled sauce-pan and cook. When done, remove from heat.
2 In another unoiled pan, roast rice until golden brown. Transfer to a mortar or blender and grind.
3 Mix meat, ground rice, pepper, lemon juice and fish sauce in a bowl. Taste and adjust flavor if necessary.
4 Add remaining salad ingredients, and mix well.
5 Arrange endive and chicory leaves on a serving dish and put meat mixture in the middle. Garnish with mint. Using the greens like a taco shell, roll up meat and eat.

Cooking meat in an unoiled pan.

Cooking rice until golden brown.

A Dinner Menu Featuring A "Steamboat" Style Main Dish

For a casual dinner party, here is a menu for
Thai style "sukiyaki".
Meat, seafood and vegetables
lightly cooked in a steamboat
at the table make for a tasty and
enjoyable evening.

Thai "Steamboat" (Sukiyaki)

This one pot meal has everything from meat, seafood, vegetables to dumplings, and noodles. Enjoy the left over soup by adding cooked rice or noodles to the broth.

Ingredients 10 servings

Dipping sauce

5 tablespoons dark soy sauce
10 tablespoons light soy sauce
3½ ounces powdered sugar
⅔ cup chili sauce
½ cup pickled garlic (or scallions)
3½ tablespoons pickled garlic juice
5-6 small coriander roots
1⅓ cups seasoning sauce
½ cup vinegar
1 tablespoon sesame oil

Soup

appropriate amounts of fish, meat, shellfish, shrimp, squid, mushrooms, rice noodles, asparagus, etc., cleaned and cut into pieces
chicken stock

Directions

1 Combine dipping sauce ingredients in a blender and blend for 20-30 seconds. Place in a saucepan and bring to a boil. Remove from heat and let cool.
2 Arrange soup ingredients on a platter.
3 Pour chicken stock into the steamboat. Add soup ingredients to the stock a little at a time and cook lightly. (Cooking time will vary depending on thickness of ingredient.) Do not over cook. Dip into sauce and eat. Continue to add ingredients and cook adding stock when necessary.
4 After all ingredients have been eaten, pour rice or noodles in remaining stock and cook lightly.

Homemade meatballs or fishballs add flavor to soup.

Sauce ingredients boiled together briefly.

Thai Spring Rolls (Papia Sod)

These Thai spring rolls combine shrimp, chicken, noodles and vegetables and are eaten with a sweet and fragrant dipping sauce.

Ingredients 10 servings

10 sheets rice paper
10 large beefsteak basil leaves
1¾ ounces mungbean noodles
1 cucumber, cut into strips
5 chicken fillets, poached and shredded
1 bunch chives, cut into ¼" lengths
10 large shrimp, heads removed, shelled and deveined
10 pieces spring onion, cut into 3" pieces
Condiments: sweet chili sauce or chili sauce

Directions

1 Soak noodles in water for 10 minutes or until soft. Add to boiling water and cook briefly. Uncurl the shrimp, being careful not to break it into pieces. Cook briefly in boiling water.
2 Slice the top of the spring onion and curl tips with the edge of a knife. Soak in cold water.
3 Dip the rice paper in warm water. Place on a paper towel and allow to soften.
4 Taking one sheet of rice paper at a time, place basil, noodles, chicken, cucumber and chives on rice paper. Add shrimp and onion. Roll up tightly, leaving the shrimp tail and curled portion of onion exposed.
5 Dip spring rolls in the sweet chili sauce and eat. (Vary chili sauce by adding vinegar to the sauce.)

Handle rice paper carefully.

Arrange shrimp and onion so that they stick out of the spring roll.

Stuffed Tomatoes (Yam Pla)

*A tuna and coconut filling makes these stuffed tomatoes
a delicious alternative.*

Ingredients 10 servings

2 cans tuna packed in water
1½ cups grated coconut
1 tablespoon ginger, thinly sliced
1 tablespoon lemon peel, thinly sliced
4 tablespoons lemon juice
1½ teaspoons salt
pinch of sugar
¼ red onion, thinly sliced
6-10 small Thai chilies, minced (or 1-2 tablespoons crushed red pepper)
10 medium tomatoes
Garnish: coriander leaves

Directions

1 Roast grated coconut in an unoiled frying pan until golden brown.
2 Cut off top quarter or fifth of tomato and remove flesh with a spoon.
3 In a bowl, combine tuna, roasted coconut, and remaining ingredients and mix well.
4 Spoon the mixture into shelled tomatoes. Garnish and serve.

Mixing tuna and other salad ingredients.

Removing flesh from tomatoes carefully to make tomato shells.

Filling tomato shells.

Thai Seasonings and Ingredients

The temperate climate of Southeast Asia produces a wealth of plants. These plants, from vegetables and fruits to spices and herbs, are all an integral part of Thai cuisine. Due to the recent popularity of Thai cooking, many of the more common ingredients are now available, if not in the oriental section of local supermarkets, then at health food stores or Asian markets. With this in mind, I have tried to arrange the recipes using ingredients that are more readily available. Where a substitution of ingredients does not affect the authenticity of the recipe, I have given alternative ingredients which are available in local markets.

Fragrant and Hot Spices

Coriander (*Bakuchi*): The leaves, stems and roots of this plant are an indispensable part of Thai cooking. It comes in both fresh and dried form.

Lemongrass *(Ta Krai)*: This plant has a strong lemon fragrance. It is used to add fragrance to soups like *tom yang kun*. It comes both fresh and in dried form.

Kaffir Lime Leaf *(Ma Khrui)*: Another name for this plant is Bergamot. It is a deeply fragrant member of the orange family and is used in soups and curries. Lime is often used as a substitute. It comes both fresh and in dried form.

Galangal *(Kha)*: This member of the ginger family has a strong fragrance. It is used to give dishes a fragrant smell. It comes both fresh and in dried form.

Rhizome *(Kra Chai)*: Another member of the ginger family, rhizome is used in fish dishes to eliminate fishy odors. It comes both fresh and in dried form.

Large Thai Chili (*Prik Chifa*): This chili is large and rather mild. It is often used to add color to dishes.

Small Thai Chili (*Prik Nu*): Said to resemble a rat's tail, this chili is the smallest and hottest of all Thai chili. The ground form of this chili is called *pon prik nu.*

Types of Seasonings

Fish Sauce (*Nam Pla*): This sauce is made by fermenting fish in salt. It is both sweet and salty and is used in almost all Thai cooking.

Light Soy Sauce (*Siew Kao*): This light soy sauce is used mostly in sautéed dishes. It is very different in flavor from dark soy sauce.

Dark Soy Sauce (*Siew Dam*): Unlike light soy sauce, this soy sauce is very thick and almost black in color. It is seasoned with sugar and various spices.

Seasoning Sauce: This Tamari soy sauce is made mostly from soy beans and is used to bring out the fragrance of dishes.

Thai Chili Sauce: Chilies and garlic make up this distinctive sauce. It is often used as a dipping sauce.

Sweet Chili Sauce *(Nam Jim Gai)*: This sweet and sour chili sauce is used on fried foods and is also a dipping sauce for meats.

Chili in Oil *(Nam Prik Pao)*: Chili, garlic and dried shrimp fried in oil make up the base of this paste. It is used in fried dishes.

Palm Sugar *(Nam Tan Pip)*: Made from palm, this sugar resembles brown sugar and is used in desserts. The distinctive flavor of this sugar goes well with coconut milk.

Shrimp Paste *(Kapi)*: Kapi, also known as blanchen, is made from salted shrimp. It is available in paste and in cubes.

Tamarind *(Ma-Kham)*: Tamarind is used to give food a tangy taste. The sticky flesh inside the pod of this tree is extracted and combined with water.

Brown Sugar: Light brown sugar is also used in Thai cooking.

Other ingredients

Coconut milk (*Ka-Thi*): Both canned and powdered coconut milk are used in curries and desserts. Canned milk must be refrigerated after opening. The thickened portion that rises to the surface of canned coconut milk is referred to as coconut cream.

Curry paste (*Nam Prik*): Four common packaged curry pastes include red, green, yellow, and panang curry paste.

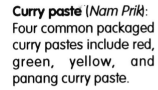

Rice flour noodles (*Kuai-Tiao Sen Lek*): Made from rice flour these noodles come in a variety of thicknesses. Though fresh noodles are available, these noodles usually come dried.

Pickled garlic (*Kra-Thiam Dong*): Pickled in a sweet vinegar, these are often used as garnish. The pickling liquid is also used in sauces.

Grated Coconut (*Ma-Phrao Khao*): Making grated coconut involves scraping the flesh of the coconut from the shell and drying it out. Luckily, grated coconut comes already packaged.

Tapioca Pearls (*Sa-khu Met Lek*): Tapioca is made from casava tubers and is used in a variety of desserts. Tapioca flour is also available.

Fried onions: These thinly sliced red onions are fried and used as garnish on noodles and salad dishes.

Fried garlic (*Krathiam Jiew*): Fried minced garlic is also used as a garnish on many different dishes.

About Thai Rice

Rice is the staple food in the Thai diet. It is served with meat, vegetables and curry dishes and also as a main dish by itself. Thai rice is of a non-glutinous long grain variety. Unlike Japanese and Chinese varieties of rice, when Thai rice is cooked it comes out firm and fluffy.

The secret of making Thai rice lies in the amount of water used during cooking. To make a pot of rice, follow these instructions.

1   Put rice in a strainer and rinse under cold water. Rinse gently since long grain rice tends to break easily..

2   Transfer to a cooking pot and add water. Water level should reach to just about one knuckle above the rice.

3   Heat until water boils. Cover and reduce to medium heat.

4   Cook for about 20 minutes or until water is completely absorbed. (It is best not to remove the cover when rice is cooking).

Postscript
by Akiko Ujike

My first introduction to the world of Thai cooking came not too long after I moved to Thailand. One evening, I happened to notice Ms. Chen, a woman who cooked for us, picnicking in the garden with some of her friends. What piqued my curiosity was not just the delicious smells that were coming from the dishes, but the enjoyable and relaxed atmosphere of the meal. Talking and laughing were just as important to the meal as the food itself. The women asked me to join them and, from the flavor and unique fragrance of the food, my adventure in Thai cooking began.

Since families in Thailand tend to be large, meals are often a very noisy and social affair. The dishes served for the meal are usually placed in the middle of the table and everyone takes what he or she wants from each dish. Condiments such as sugar, vinegar, chili and fish sauce are served at each meal and everyone seasons their food to their own liking. Compared to American and European style meals, Thai meals are relaxed and less concerned with form or order of dishes.

The recipes in this book have been arranged using the Thai ingredients that are generally available in supermarkets or Asian markets. In some cases, I have given alternatives for common Thai ingredients. These include using lemon or lime instead of tamarind juice, or crushed red pepper in the place of Thai chili, etc.

It is my sincere hope that the thirty recipes presented in this book will give you a taste of the unique and delicious flavors that make up Thai cooking.

Akiko Ujike was born in Tokyo in 1943. She moved to Thailand in 1967 and lived there for two years. After returning to Tokyo, she studied Thai cooking through the Bangkok restaurant 'Busarakamu' under Chief Chef Bunchu. Currently, Ms. Ujike works as a Thai food coordinator, develops menus and also does volunteer work with Thai children. She also instructs cooks on Thai cooking.

Ms. Akiko has also written pieces including "My Thai Cooking" for Shibata Shoten Publishing Co.